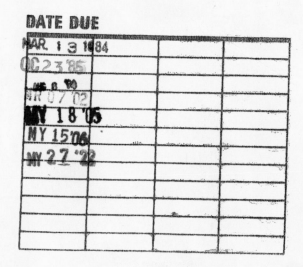

Famous Names
in
SOCCER

Jim Bebbington

Wayland

To Sam and Alex

Other books in this series

Famous Names in Medicine
Famous Names in Crime
Famous Names in Space Exploration
Famous Names in World Exploration
Famous Names in Music
Famous Names in Science
Famous Names in Sport
Famous Names in Popular Music
Famous Names in Films
Famous Names in Seafaring
Famous Names in Aviation
Famous Names in Motoring
Famous Names in Warfare
Famous Names in Invention

ISBN 0 85340 790 8
© COPYRIGHT 1980 WAYLAND PUBLISHERS LTD
FIRST PUBLISHED IN 1980 BY
WAYLAND PUBLISHERS LTD
49 LANSDOWNE PLACE, HOVE
EAST SUSSEX, BN3 1HF, ENGLAND
TYPESET BY COMPUTACOMP (UK) LTD, FORT WILLIAM, SCOTLAND
PRINTED AND BOUND IN GREAT BRITAIN
AT THE PITMAN PRESS, BATH

Contents

Other famous soccer players are included in
Famous Names in Sport

Bill Shankly

The father of the modern Reds

Bill Shankly is best known for his achievements in soccer as manager of Liverpool F.C., England's most successful post-war soccer club.

It was as a wing half for Preston North End in the late 1930s that Bill Shankly first came to prominence. He won his first international cap for Scotland in 1938 in the match against 'the auld enemy' England. The next year he won four more caps before the war put an end to his international playing career.

In the 1950s Shankly turned to management and had experience at Workington, Carlisle and Huddersfield Town. In December 1959 he moved to Anfield and set about rebuilding the Liverpool team.

Probably his cleverest move was to retain the training staff, including manager Bob Paisley, who were at the club when he joined. The two players bought to lift the Reds from the Second Division (1961–62) were Ian St. John and the towering defender, Ron Yeats. Later came Ray Clemence, Kevin Keegan, and Ray Kennedy. The picture shows Shankly surrounded by fans after Liverpool won the F.A. Cup in 1973.

Shank's ability to motivate his players was his greatest attribute. It takes skill and organization to win cups and championships, but it takes great motivation to go on winning and winning. 'There are two first-class teams on Merseyside,' said Shankly, 'Liverpool and Liverpool Reserves!' The quality of the Liverpool squad and its ability to sustain form over more than sixty games a season is tribute to Bill Shankly, his assistants and his development of Melwood into the best training ground in the land.

Brian Clough

The magical motivator

There was a time when Brian Clough appeared so regularly on television that he seemed to be more a television personality than a soccer manager. However, there is no denying his achievement in bringing Derby County from Division 2 to the League Championship between 1967 and 1972. Clough's forthright attitudes have brought him fame, fans and foes, but his players respect and work hard for him.

There is a charisma about Brian Clough which constantly brings him before the public eye. As a player he had a phenomenal goalscoring record before a severe leg fracture brought his career to an end at the age of twenty-seven.

He began his management career as manager with Hartlepool United, and then moved to Derby County to bring them a joyous period of success. However, he fell out with the Derby board and left in spite of protests from the players. In November 1973 he and Peter Taylor, his aide from Hartlepool and Derby, joined Brighton and Hove Albion. The following summer Clough left Taylor at Brighton and joined Leeds United, but this 'marriage' lasted only forty-eight days, and Clough left the game for a few months before joining Nottingham Forest.

This set Forest alight! Some skilful team building brought Forest promotion to Division I in 1977. The restored Clough/Taylor partnership then steered the team to the League Championship in 1978 and a second successive League Cup triumph. In 1979 they were runners-up in the league, but added Trevor Francis to their team and won the European Cup. In 1980 Forest repeated their European Cup success. What a tribute to Clough's ability as manager and motivator!

Phil Woosnam

The New World's Welsh wizard!

Farmer's son and physics graduate, Phil Woosnam is the lynch-pin in the establishment of professional soccer in North America. By his dedication and dynamism he has lifted the North American Soccer League (N.A.S.L.) to a level where soccer players from all over the world are delighted to play.

Phil first made his name in soccer as forward in the Welsh Under 15 Schoolboys XI in 1946–47. He quickly developed his skills, and played both as an amateur and as a professional for the full national team. He was one of the few Football League players at that time who also had an academic background, having graduated in 1953.

Following his university days, Woosnam became a teacher in London and played for Orient. In 1958 he decided to become a full-time professional player, and played for West Ham and Arsenal for the next twelve years. His teaching experience and excellence as a player helped him to become an accomplished coach, and in 1964 he became staff coach of the English Football Association.

Two years later Woosnam crossed the Atlantic and settled in the U.S.A. to take up his appointment as general manager and coach of the N.A.S.L. team, Atlanta Chiefs. Even he could hardly have predicted the massive upsurge of interest in soccer in the States. In 1968 Atlanta Chiefs won the N.A.S.L. championship, Woosnam was named 'coach of the year' and appointed coach to the U.S. World Cup team. Since 1971 he has been the Commissioner of an N.A.S.L. which has boasted Pelé, Bobby Moore, George Best and Franz Beckenbauer. Soccer in North America truly owes its success to Phil Woosnam's vision and application.

Gordon Banks

The greatest goalie ever

One save from a Pelé close-range header in the 1970 World Cup Final symbolized all that was brilliant about Gordon Banks' goalkeeping. Perfectly poised and with complete concentration, Banks watched the situation as it developed, and when the centre came across on to the head of Pelé, he hurled himself to his right to deflect the powerful, well-directed effort from the star black striker.

Banks first hit the headlines while playing for Leicester City. His sound positioning and excellent reading of the game made him a certainty for international honours, and in 1966 he achieved the highest soccer honour of all, a World Cup winner's medal. He was the cornerstone of the triumph, inspiring his fellow defenders throughout the tournament.

Banks was first capped in 1963, and conceded only 57 goals in 73 international appearances. Between 1959 and 1972 he played nearly 500 games in the First Division in the English League and was the popular hero of the fans at Filbert Street, Leicester, and from 1967 at the Victoria Ground, Stoke.

It was as goalkeeper for Stoke City and England that Gordon Banks was awarded the OBE in 1970, and was voted Footballer of the Year in 1972. But 1972 was also the year when success turned into tragedy. One Sunday in October Banks was involved in a serious car crash. His injuries resulted in the loss of effective sight in one eye. In a trice Gordon Banks' reign as the best keeper in the world was over.

There is, however, a happy postscript and another award. In 1977 Banks played for the North American Soccer League with Fort Lauderdale Strikers and was the league's 'goalkeeper of the year'.

Ivo Viktor

The consistent custodian

As goalkeeper for Dukla Prague and for the Czech national team, Ivo Viktor displayed both soundness and consistency, together with the brilliantly spectacular saves that continental keepers pull off when a goal seems certain.

Viktor joined Dukla Prague, a Czech army team, in 1963 and by 1964–65 had become the automatic first choice in goal. Dukla Prague won the Czech Cup that season and in 1965–66 won the league and cup double. It was in 1966 that Viktor made his international debut. The match was in Rio de Janeiro at the huge Maracana stadium against Brazil. Viktor played well, but was powerless to prevent Pelé scoring twice to give Brazil a 2–1 victory. Viktor's second cap was at Wembley in England, and here he really established himself as Czechoslovakia's number one keeper with a convincing performance in a 0–0 draw. In a career of more than 400 matches in top class football Viktor has never once been cautioned by a referee — a distinction which all too few players can claim.

The highlight of Viktor's career came in the 1976 European Championship. Czechoslovakia was a somewhat surprising qualifier for the final stages, but once there showed plenty of flair and determination. With Viktor in commanding form behind a defence inspired by Dobias and Capkovic, they defeated the great Dutch team 3–1 to meet West Germany in the final. As World Champions, West Germany were very much the favourites, but Viktor and his colleagues won on penalties after the match had been drawn 2–2. This achievement plus receiving the Czech Footballer of the Year award no less than five times are the highlights of Viktor's great career.

13

Franz Beckenbauer

The Kaiser

The first thing you notice about truly great sportsmen is the amount of time they always seem to have. No soccer player has ever seemed more leisurely or more effective than Franz Beckenbauer. He appears nonchalant and arrogant when he traps the ball in a defensive situation, casually sidesteps a challenge and brings the ball away from a dangerous position before setting his own team on the move. The style has always been the same, yet the apparent slowness is deceptive. In his heyday with Bayern Munich and as captain of West Germany, Beckenbauer was seldom beaten for speed and rarely harried into bungling a clearance or kicking the ball wildly upfield without trying to place it to a colleague. Today, playing for New York Cosmos, his vast experience and perfect positioning save his legs.

Beckenbauer gained his nickname 'The Kaiser' not only because he was the key player for his club and country, but also because he was influential in selecting players for the team. He was able to share his soccer knowledge and experience with West German team manager, Helmut Schoen, and together they took the West German team to the 1966 World Cup Final (lost to England 2–4) and to a 2–1 victory in 1974 against Holland.

Under Beckenbauer's splendid leadership Bayern Munich won the European Cup in 1974, 1975 and 1976, (having won the European Cup Winners Cup in 1967), and went on to become World Club Champions in 1976 to cap their European hat-trick. Franz Beckenbauer played in all these finals and in every one his cool example was a vital part of the victory.

John Charles

The gentle giant of Wales

When John Charles went to Italy to play for Juventus, the Italians christened him 'King Charles'. However, he is more widely known as the 'gentle giant' of soccer.

He joined Swansea Town (now City) in 1946 and made his league debut in 1949 at the age of seventeen. It was with Leeds United that he made his early reputation. Combining height, powerful physique, surprising balance and turn of speed he became a commanding player both in defence and attack.

In international soccer he led Wales to great heights of achievements including the 1955–56 Home International Championships, when Wales defeated England 2–1 at Ninian Park, Cardiff, and came within an ace of winning the championship itself. Under John Charles' inspired leadership Wales reached the finals of the World Cup in Sweden in 1958. In spite of some vicious tackling by their opponents Wales drew 1–1 with Hungary and defeated them 2–1 in the replay. John Charles was badly injured in the replay and was unable to play in the final in which the valiant Welsh were so narrowly defeated 1–0 by a Pelé goal for Brazil. Perhaps the result would have been different if Charles had been able to play.

John Charles settled easily into the Juventus team, quickly gaining the respect of the Italian fans. With the Welshman as their star player Juventus won three Italian League Championships and twice won the Italian cup. This period was the climax of John Charles' career. When he returned to Leeds he had passed his peak, but returned briefly to Italy to play for Roma. He then moved to Cardiff City and finally to Hereford United in the Southern League. His love of the game and gentle enthusiasm continue to inspire others.

Osvaldo Ardiles

The classic midfield player

Whilst much of the glamour of Argentina's 1978 World Cup victory surrounded such players as Mario Kempes, Daniel Passerella, and team manager Cesar Luis Menotti, the great driving force from midfield was Osvaldo Ardiles.

After the World Cup tournament, Tottenham Hotspur's manager, Keith Burkenshaw, brought off a spectacular deal in signing both Ardiles and his fellow Argentine international, Ricardo Villa. From the first match Ardiles — 'Ossie' to the fans — became Spur's key player. Tiny in height and build, but tough in combat and hard to knock off the ball, Ardiles is the springboard from which most of Spur's attacks are launched. When Spurs played him further forward Ardiles scored some significant goals — none more so than the coolly taken shot by which Spurs put Manchester United out of the 1979–80 F.A. Cup.

It is a great tribute to Ardiles that he settled so quickly to Football League play. The hurly burly of English league soccer goes on remorselessly through the depths of winter when the grounds are frequently waterlogged or covered in frost and snow. Not only did Ardiles cope with such alien conditions, but he has also mastered the cynical tackles designed to reduce his influence on matches.

His ability is best seen when he runs at massed defences and sidesteps tackles before setting up perfectly weighted passes for colleagues running into space. His ball control and body swerve are magical, and his bravery in taking hard knocks without resorting to petulant retaliation is admirable. There is little doubt that Ardiles has had more impact on English soccer than any other 'imported' player in the past five years.

Eusebio

'The Black Panther'

Of all the excellent players in Portuguese soccer during the 1960s, none was greater than Eusebio, an impudent marksman known affectionately as 'the Black Panther'.

Eusebio has often been compared with Pelé and, undeniably, they have been the greatest black players to date in world soccer. Like Pelé, Eusebio was born in abject poverty. He arrived on the Portuguese soccer scene from Lourenco Marques Sporting Club where he was a young teenage star.

Benfica, Portugal's leading club side, became the home club of Eusebio, but only after months of bitter argument with their rivals, Sporting Lisbon, who claimed that they had a prior right to Eusebio's services. Eusebio announced his arrival by scoring a second half hat-trick when he came on for Benfica as a substitute in a match against Santos in an international club tournament in Paris. He made his debut for Portugal in 1961 and soon earned a reputation for scoring spectacular goals.

It was in the 1966 World Cup Final in England that Eusebio really hit the headlines. He hassled and harried the Hungarians to a 3–1 defeat, crashed in a great goal to dismiss Bulgaria, and hammered home a lethal volley to destroy Brazil. But nothing could compare with his performance against North Korea. This diminutive team led Portugal 3–0 after twenty minutes and their agile display had the crowd at Goodison Park and the Portuguese players gasping in disbelief. One man set himself to put things right — Eusebio. By half-time he had scored a solo goal and then slammed home a penalty kick. In the second half he doubled the score with a crashing volley and another penalty kick, and laid on a fifth goal scored by Augusto. Here Eusebio puts a goal past Gordon Banks during practice.

Trevor Francis

Million pounds man!

The European Cup Final of 1979 was a very dull match. F.C. Malmo, the Swedish champions, were underdogs and played in terror of being humiliated by English champions, Nottingham Forest. Only one player raised his game above the mediocrity which surrounded him.

The outstanding moment was the solitary goal by which Forest won the match. It was a fearless diving header scored by the man of the match, Trevor Francis. That goal and Trevor's performance showed why Brian Clough, the Forest manager, had been willing to pay £1 million to Birmingham City to acquire the services of this brilliant striker. It was an immense burden to carry the tag of being Britain's first million pound transfer fee player, but any doubts among the Forest supporters or tentativeness by Francis himself were dispelled in this classic display.

Before joining Nottingham Forest, Trevor Francis played all his senior football for Birmingham City, for whom he made nearly 300 league appearances.

Francis must have found it odd to be the million pound reserve player when he arrived at Forest. But Brian Clough was intent on moulding his star player into the Forest system before making him automatic choice for the number ten shirt.

The 1979 European Cup Final unlocked a whole string of exciting performances both for Forest and for England. Classic goals by Francis against Dynamo Berlin and against Ajax took Forest to their second successive European Cup Final. As the England team fought through to the finals of the European Nations Cup, Francis proved himself a brave and brilliant striker and a finisher of clinical precision.

Pelé

The master

Of all the famous soccer players in the world Pelé stands alone. The wealth of his achievements is difficult to believe. He played in the finals of the World Cup on three occasions, scoring twice in the final for Brazil against Sweden when he was only seventeen. He made his international debut at the age of sixteen and went on to win 110 caps for his country. Playing for Santos in Brazil he won every possible club honour. In 1975 when he left Santos to join New York Cosmos in a $2^1/_2$ million dollar deal, he uplifted American soccer to an unprecedented level of popularity. He scored 1,271 goals in his career including 91 hat-tricks.

Pelé was born in 1941 and was brought up in extreme poverty in the small Brazilian town of Bauru. At fifteen years of age he went for trials at the Santos soccer club. International acclaim and popularity have done little to change Pelé's basic modesty, although he now has a charisma that grows with success.

Along with Muhammad Ali, Pelé has become the best-known face in sport. He has visited more than eighty countries, met ten kings, five emperors, seventy presidents, more than forty heads of state as well as two popes. In Nigeria a two-day truce was declared in the war with Biafra to enable both sides to watch him play — such was the status of Pelé.

On the field Pelé had speed, acceleration, control, brilliant heading and shooting power, and above all wonderful vision in seeing openings for goals and well-positioned colleagues.

The picture shows a jubilant Pelé (centre) after scoring for Brazil in the 1970 World Cup Final.

Johan Cruyff

The golden orange

Johan Cruyff — the golden boy of European soccer in the 1970s — was the man responsible for the emergence of Ajax, the Amsterdam team, as champions of Europe.

Born in 1947 in Amsterdam, Johan Cruyff had style, verve and burning ambition tempered by an inherent shyness. The shyness, however, disappeared once the football was at his feet. His balance, control and powerful shooting brought him rapidly to the attention not only of Ajax, but also to a first cap for his country in 1965 at the age of eighteen. He was the delight of his youthful contemporaries, but ended his international debut, against Czechoslovakia, in disgrace. Having withstood several foul tackles which the referee ignored, he rudely addressed an official and was sent off. This made him less than popular with the Dutch selection board, but Cruyff soon worked his way back into the team as it became a major force in world soccer.

Goals flowed and Cruyff scored 167 times for Ajax between 1964 and 1973. With Cruyff as captain, Ajax won the European Cup in 1971, 1972 and 1973. Cruyff also became captain of the Dutch national team and was voted European Footballer of the Year three times. In 1973 he shook the Ajax fans by moving to Spain to take up an enormous offer from F.C. Barcelona. They not only paid a vast sum to Ajax, but also guaranteed Cruyff an income of £400,000 spread over three years. The deal paid off for Barcelona became Spanish league champions in 1974 and won the cup in 1978.

Despite the disappointment of suffering defeat in successive World Cup Finals in 1974 and 1978, Cruyff will forever be 'the golden one' to his Dutch supporters.

Kevin Keegan

Superstar

Keegan began his spectacular soccer career with lowly Scunthorpe United, moved via the dizzy heights of Liverpool F.C. and H.S.V. Hamburg and has now returned to the relative calm of The Dell at Southampton. Throughout his career he has shown himself to be an excellent footballer, a good learner, an ambassador of the game, and a well-adjusted family man able to withstand the pressures of being a superstar.

Captain of England, European Footballer of the Year, European Cup finalist for both Liverpool and H.S.V. Hamburg, Kevin Keegan has certainly had his share of glittering prizes since Bill Shankly took him to Anfield.

The signing of Keegan must rate as Shankly's master stroke as manager of Liverpool. The qualities that Shankly recognized in Keegan are those which have taken him to the very top in world soccer. Keegan combines ability on the ball with a restless energy and burning determination to succeed. He has excellent vision on the field of play, spots openings quickly and has the ability to exploit them by dashing through to score himself or put through a telling pass for another player to apply the finishing touch. At Liverpool he had an almost telepathic partnership with John Toshack and the pair of them scored with great regularity.

Kevin Keegan's great abilities as a footballer were probably best demonstrated in the 1977 European Cup Final when he was the inspiration of Liverpool's fine victory over Borussia Münchengladbach. His courageous and skilful play simply destroyed Berti Vogts, who was probably the best close marker in the game. After great success in the Bundesliga Keegan has made a welcome return to English soccer with Southampton.

Tom Finney

The Preston plumber

Equally at home on either wing and occasionally called upon to play inside or centre-forward, Tom Finney was the complete footballer. He could not only dribble as effectively as the legendary Stanley Matthews, but could also shoot powerfully with either foot and was a surprisingly strong header of the ball.

Finney scored 187 goals in 431 games for Preston North End and is the only winger to have scored more than 30 goals for England in international matches. He collected 76 international caps, having made his England debut in 1946.

As a 'two-footed' player, Finney was equally dangerous on whichever wing he was playing. He could centre the ball 'inch perfect' with either foot, and centre-forwards such as Tommy Lawton, Stan Mortensen and Nat Lofthouse scored a hatful of goals thanks to Finney's finesse.

There is no doubting Finney's natural talents, but it was practice, practice and more practice that enabled him to maximize these talents. He was naturally left-footed, but trained for hours with a plimsoll on his strong left foot and a boot on his weaker right until both were equally powerful. His other great virtue was loyalty and he remained a Preston North End player for twenty-three years.

Probably his saddest moment was in 1954 when Preston lost 3–2 to West Bromwich Albion in the F.A. Cup Final and Finney, then the club captain, had a poor game. Among many happy moments in soccer, his own favourite was when he scored four goals in a 5–3 victory over Portugal in 1950.

In those days Tom Finney earned the maximum wage of £20 per week. What would a player of his calibre earn today? Certainly he would not have needed his trade as a plumber!

Bobby Charlton

The unassuming hero

Bobby Charlton spent all his professional soccer career with Manchester United, but played both his first and last league games in London. His league debut for United was, fittingly, at Charlton where he introduced himself with two goals. He signed off seventeen seasons later, in 1973, before a full house at Chelsea.

Charlton joined Manchester United in 1953 after becoming an English schoolboy international. By the time he was nineteen he went to Wembley as a member of the United team which lost the 1957 F.A. Cup Final 1–2 to Aston Villa. He also survived the horrors of the Munich air crash in 1958 when seventeen United players met their deaths. In 1958 he made his England debut against Scotland at Hampden Park, heralding his international arrival with a spectacularly volleyed goal — the sort for which he became famous.

But the mid-1960s were Bobby's really great years. His play matured and, whether playing on the wing or scheming from midfield, he continued to score a hatful of great goals. He was the idol of Old Trafford when United won the F.A. Cup in 1963 and the League Championship in 1965. In 1966 he was the vital creative talent of England's World Cup triumph. He scored a magnificent goal against Mexico in England's opening match of the final stages and netted two more against Portugal in the semi-final. In 1967 Manchester United were league champions again and followed this by winning the 1968 European Cup Final.

When his playing days ended Bobby was manager of Preston North End for a short while, but left to become a public relations figure for the game.

George Best

The wayward wizard

Belfast-born George Best joined Manchester United at the age of fifteen. He made a dramatic debut as a professional player in the 1963–64 season against Sunderland, scoring a last gasp equalizer for United. Within a year he had become the centre of attraction wherever United played. He was slight of build, but fleet of foot, and his footwork and ball control were a delight to watch. He skilfully opened up defences and, given the chance of a shot at goal, was a deadly marksman.

His main problem at this stage was withstanding challenges from defenders who were sick of being belittled by his devastating dribbling skills. George somehow seemed to encourage such challenges by his taunting attitude, beating the same man twice and all this with his socks nonchalantly round his ankles and no shin pads for protection. However, he did have quite a temper and would kick back at defenders.

But there was no denying his natural soccer talents. He was first capped for Northern Ireland in 1964 and later that year scored his first international goal — against Scotland at Hampden Park. In 1968 he played a vital role when Manchester United won the European Cup and he was voted European Player of the Year.

From then on George's career fell apart. He became involved in too much high living, failed to turn up for training, was sacked by Manchester United, played Southern League football for Dunstable Town in 1973, and then played for several North American Soccer League teams. A comeback first with Fulham and then with Hibernian promised better, but sadly George Best was still unable to balance his life style and his prodigous soccer talents.

Alfredo di Stefano

The Real Madrid grandmaster

When Real Madrid were the undisputed kings of European soccer in the late 1950s, their many international stars included a centre-forward whose skills could open up even the best of defences. This most creative of players was Alfredo di Stefano.

Di Stefano did not simply create goals, but frequently moved forward quickly from his deep-lying position to take advantage of an opening to score. This talent was never more brilliantly demonstrated than in the 1960 European Cup Final when Real beat Eintracht of Frankfurt 7–3 at Hampden Park. Di Stefano ran through from the half-way line, swerving past and sidestepping defenders along the way before emphatically whipping the ball past the goalkeeper.

Born in Argentina, di Stefano was a commanding player in more ways than one! He saw himself as the general at Real Madrid and was very much involved in decisions as to who should play in the team. The picture shows di Stefano (right) in training.

It is hard to think of di Stefano without reference to his Hungarian co-star at Real, Ferenc Puskas, the prolific goal-scorer. Their deep friendship and soccer understanding brought out the best in both of them as Real had an undefeated run at home from February 1957 which ran for eight years.

In spite of the value of the explosive left-foot shooting of Puskas and the great contributions of such players as Kopa, the French international, and Gento, the Spanish winger, di Stefano was surely the greatest player of his generation. He was the hub of Real's every move with his close control and shrewd distribution. With di Stefano as manager, Valencia F.C. won the European Cup Winners Cup in 1980.

Alan Ball

The red-haired dynamo

In many ways Alan Ball typifies all that is good about English soccer. His tremendous work rate and enthusiasm have never flagged since he made his league debut with Blackpool in the 1962–63 season. Once he had learned to curb the explosive temper which marred his early career, Alan Ball became a player on which any budding midfield footballer could model himself. Alan's father was also a professional footballer, and later a manager, so it was not surprising that Alan junior wanted to play. He originally joined Bolton Wanderers, but became an apprentice with Blackpool when he was seventeen. In the 1963–64 season he became Blackpool's top scorer, and in 1965 was capped for England against Yugoslavia and Sweden.

1966 was a great year for Alan. He played in four of England's six World Cup matches, and was a star performer in the victory over West Germany in the final, when his energy and zest for the game helped inspire the team during extra time. That summer he transferred to Everton, for whom he was a regular goalscorer. In the 1970 World Cup Finals in Mexico Alan was a vital member of the England team. Even in the intense heat and the rarified atmosphere of Mexico his work rate was undiminished but, on his return to league soccer, his form suddenly declined. Everton were not playing well either, and the outcome was that Alan was transferred to Arsenal, where he was a great asset, as he was later at Southampton.

Alan Ball also captained the England team briefly, giving unselfish leadership and service. It will be interesting to follow his new career in the managerial chain at Bloomfield Road, Blackpool, where he began his league career. The picture shows Alan Ball (right) with Osvaldo Ardiles.

Denis Law

Scotland's deadliest ever marksman

The arm aloft, the hand held high, the broad grin — Denis Law salutes yet another goal for club or country. This was a familiar sight on British soccer grounds through the 1960s and 1970s when Law had an electrifying presence on the field.

He first ran on to the English soccer scene with Huddersfield Town. Immediately he started scoring goals frequently and enthusiastically. Having become a Huddersfield hero, he moved to Maine Road to do wonders for Manchester City. He was like quicksilver in the goal area, darting into gaps to snatch up half chances, or explosively leaping high above much bigger defenders to flash the ball into the net with a dramatic header.

Denis Law's speed, elusiveness and daring in or around the goal area were legendary, and woe betide any goalkeeper who fumbled a shot when Denis was around. The keeper would have little or no time to recover before Denis had whipped the loose ball into the back of the net.

Goalscoring in Italian soccer has always been difficult because of the very tight defensive play of Italian teams, but Denis still managed to find the net regularly in his spell with Torino. No matter how many opponents were used to intimidate him Denis continued to find the gaps, shrug the tackles, break clear of the shirt-holders and obstructions, and be on hand to score. When Denis came back from Italy to play for Manchester United he became a god at Old Trafford and always gave of his enthusiastic best.

Denis Law was at his peak playing in the blue jersey for Scotland and scored thirty goals in fifty-five appearances for his country. He now works for the BBC as a soccer commentator where his analysis of matches is much appreciated.

Gerd Müller

The goal machine

It took Gerd Müller less than six years to overtake the German international goalscoring record established by Uwe Seeler over twelve seasons. In his first fifty internationals Müller scored no less than fifty goals.

Like Seeler, Müller is a short man, but he has that amazing springheeled ability to compete with tall defenders for high centres across the goal. His goalscoring feats for Bayern Munich in the Bundesliga and in the various European Cups are legion. No matter how tight the defensive play of the opposition, Gerd Müller had the skill to wriggle clear and whip the loose ball or quick pass into the net. He was a nightmare for goalkeepers and back four defenders. The picture shows

Müller (right) notching up another goal for Bayern.

In the 1970 World Cup Finals in Mexico Müller combined with Seeler to form an almost lethal spearhead for West Germany. Müller was the tournament's leading goalscorer with ten goals to his credit. This achievement, against packed defences, included hat-tricks against Bulgaria and Peru and, as no Englishman needs reminding, the extra-time quarter-final winner against England. In the 1974 World Cup tournament Müller only scored four goals — but the fourth goal was the winner against Holland in the final itself.

It is interesting to reflect that Gerd Müller was turned down by Nuremburg F.C. and by T.S.V. Munich before he signed for Bayern Munich. His signing for Bayern Munich only came about when the president of the club was so sure of Müller's abilities and potential that he overruled the then manager and completed the signing. How Nuremburg and T.S.V. Munich must have wished they had more forceful presidents!

Diego Maradona

The Argentine whizz-kid

Many of the stars in this book have reached greatness only when experience has been added to their raw talent but, like Pelé before him, one South American has emerged in his teens as a superstar and already has enough wealth to keep him in comfort for the rest of his life.

Diego Maradona's prowess and renown are such that he is mentioned in the same breath as Pelé, Cruyff and Keegan. At the age of nineteen he is the centre of attraction in the Argentine team which has begun its rebuilding for the 1982 World Cup Finals. In 1978 he just missed a place in Argentina's victorious World Cup team, but he is now the inspiration for their quest to retain the Championship.

The world's wealthiest clubs would dearly love to have Maradona in their teams, but Argentina has refused him permission to be transferred abroad. Barcelona, who it is rumoured were prepared to spend three million pounds to sign him on, will have to wait until after the 1982 World Cup Finals.

It is an ironic fact that in 1978 he was nearly signed by Sheffield United, which he saw as an opportunity of providing money for his family. His home club, Argentinos Juniors of Buenos Aires, finally acquired sponsorship from a bank which enabled the club to pay Maradona enough to keep him.

He is a short, stocky, immensely strong player. His brilliant ball control, amazing acceleration and strength in carrying the ball through tackles give him the opportunity to bring into play his powerful swerving shots especially from his left foot. All the signs are that Diego Maradona — currently the world's youngest soccer superstar — has a great future.

Glossary

Cap Each player taking part in an international match is awarded a cap with a badge commemorating the game. Hence the expression 'to be capped for your country'.

Debut A player's first game for the team.

European Cup Winners Cup A knock-out tournament played between European teams who won the national F.A. Cup trophies in the previous season.

F.A. Cup Final The final of the English Football Association knockout cup competition which is played every year at Wembley.

Hat-trick This expression can apply to three wins in a row by a team or to three goals scored by one player in a match.

Home International Championship The annual competition, operated on a league basis, between the national teams of England, Scotland, Wales and Northern Ireland.

Player of the Year The player voted by sports journalists to be the outstanding player of the season. In England the players themselves vote their choice for the 'Players' Player of the Year' award.

Signing The signing of the contract of employment by a player joining a new club.

Transfer fee The amount of money paid by one soccer club to another to secure the transfer of a player from that club to the purchaser.

World Cup The premier international soccer tournament which takes place every four years. Geographical groups of countries compete to produce finalists, and the final stages are played on a knockout basis.

Reading List

Soccer by Jim Bebbington (Wayland 1980)

The Young Player's Guide to Soccer by Jim Bebbington (David & Charles 1979)

Rothman's Football Yearbook (Queen Anne Press)

The Guinness Book of Soccer Facts and Feats by Jack Rollin (Guinness Superlatives 1978)

The ABC of Soccer Sense by Tommy Docherty (Batsford 1978)

The Story of Soccer by Martin Tyler (Marshall Cavendish 1976)

The Big Matches by Brian Moore and Martin Tyler (Queen Anne Press 1980)

Success in Football by Mike Smith (John Murray 1978)

Picture Acknowledgements

Duncan Raban/Allsport Photographic 18; John Topham Picture Library 10, 15; Keystone Press Agency 30, 42–3; Sport and General 8, 36; Sporting Pictures (UK) Ltd. 7, 39, 41, 44; Syndication International 4, 13, 17, 21, 23, 24, 26, 29, 33, 34.

Index